THE HEYDAY OF OLD OAK COMMON AND ITS LOCOMOTIVES

First published 1993

ISBN 0 7110 2143 0

IAN ALLAN
Publishing

Terminal House   Shepperton TW17 8AS
Telephone: 0932 228950
Fax: 0932 247520   Telex: 929806 IALLAN G

Phototypesetting/printing: Ian Allan Printing Ltd at their works at Coombelands in Runnymede, England

Front cover:
The big Westbourne Park goods depot appears in this view of 'Castle' No 7005 *Sir Edward Elgar* heading an up express of rather assorted stock. No 7005 was built in 1946 as *Lamphey Castle* and renamed after the famous Worcestershire composer in August 1957. The goods yard contains a typical mix of vans and open wagons and, as one would expect in a September 1960 view, the majority are vacuum brake fitted vehicles permitting their use in fast freight services. *R. C. Riley*

Back cover:
Gleaming 'County' class 4-6-0 No 1009 *County of Carmarthen* stands at the Ranelagh Bridge servicing point outside Paddington, having been turned ready for a down service. The 'County' wears the early style tender emblem, while on the left another of the class may be glimpsed in the original 'mixed traffic' black livery. *R. C. Riley*

Chris Leigh & R. C. Riley

Introduction

Old Oak Common. To a Western enthusiast the words have a magic ring to them. They are matched only by Swindon, Brunel, Paddington and Churchward in their significance. Old Oak Common was the Great Western Railway's main locomotive depot in London. It could easily have been called Acton, or perhaps Wormwood Scrubs or North Pole, as is its new neighbour, the servicing depot for international trains. Somehow none of those would have had the same magic nor conjured up the same, quite erroneous, rural picture.

Old Oak served the needs of Paddington. It was the largest depot on the GWR and provided not only top-link express passenger locomotives but also express freight engines, goods engines, shunters, local trip-working power and carriage stock pilots for Paddington.

The new depot opened on 17 March 1906, having taken nearly four years in construction. It was designed by Chief Mechanical Engineer George Jackson Churchward as the prototype for a standardised major MPD, in which the main covered accommodation contained a number of turntables. At Old Oak there were four, arranged in a square pattern. Wolverhampton Stafford Road was the next largest with three, but most had only one or two and the pattern was confined to a few major depots. Elsewhere, straight sheds remained the norm and the GWR built no true roundhouses. The turntables were 65ft in diameter with underhung girders and the turntable pits were boarded over.

Old Oak Common was provided with a substantial repair shop in which 11 out of 12 repair roads were accessed by a

traverser immediately in front of the building. This repair shop became known as 'the factory', a title which it retains to this day, as one of the last surviving buildings. It still functions as a repair shop for diesel locomotives but at the time of writing, is under threat of imminent closure.

The structures at Old Oak were typical of GWR architecture of the period, being constructed of red brick embellished with round-nosed engineers' blues, and roofed in slate. The coaling stage was a very large version of the standard GWR type. Due to the soft nature of the Welsh coal it could not be dropped from the high hopper coaling towers favoured by other railways. The GWR coaled from small 'tubs' running on rails carried out over the locomotive tender, and tipped by hand. These were loaded direct from coal wagons which were pushed up an incline to reach the level of the tubs. At Old Oak the ramp was 1 in 50 and the coaling tubs could handle two or three locomotives either side. The whole coaling stage was contained in a brick-built structure which carried on its top the enormous 290,000 gallon water tank.

Under the GWR system the code for Old Oak Common was 'PDN', though from time to time 'OOC' would appear in the traditional GWR location on the leading edge of the footplating. As the main shed in No 1 District it took the code 81A under BR, the '8' signifying Western Region, '1' the London District, and 'A' the premier shed in that district.

Old Oak Common was equipped to deal with oil-fired locomotives during the postwar coal shortage and since suitable oil supplies were already on hand, the two gas turbine locomotives were also serviced there. With the coming of dieselisation, Old Oak was again in the forefront and from 1958 faced the difficulty of coping with sensitive diesel traction alongside all the dirt and contamination associated with a busy steam depot. Inevitably developments began quite quickly to change the depot for its new traction, with the result that the steam allocation was reduced and work began in 1964 on demolishing the main shed to provide 'straight' sheds for the diesels and adjacent coaching stock servicing areas. In March 1965, almost to the day 59 years after it opened, Old Oak Common's remaining steam locomotives were transferred away. Most went to Southall, but No 8486 went to Bath and

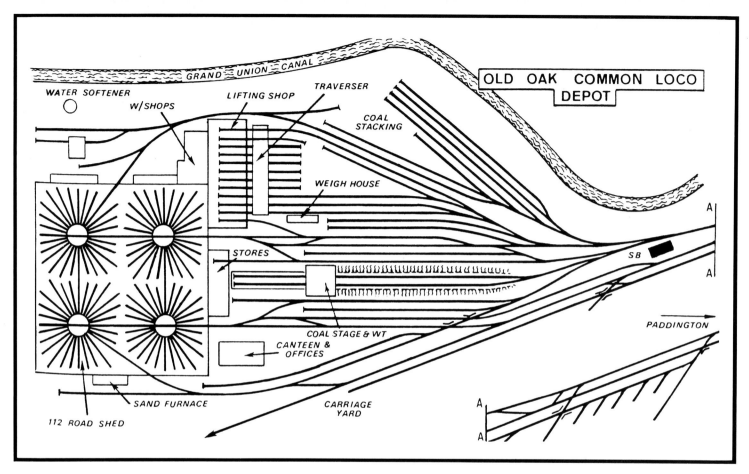

WATER SOFTENER
W/SHOPS
LIFTING SHOP
TRAVERSER
GRAND UNION CANAL
OLD OAK COMMON LOCO DEPOT
COAL STACKING
WEIGH HOUSE
STORES
SB
A | A
COAL STAGE & WT
CANTEEN & OFFICES
PADDINGTON
SAND FURNACE
CARRIAGE YARD
112 ROAD SHED
A
A

No 9405 to Bristol Barrow Road, for example. The transfers were dated three weeks ending 27 March 1965 and the last locomotives were all '57xx' and '94xx' pannier tanks.

From that time onwards, Old Oak Common remained a major diesel traction depot. Only one turntable was left, now out in the open, and the depot had a large allocation of diesel-hydraulics, later adding Brush Type 4s (Class 47s). Later still, as the hydraulics were phased out, Class 31 and Class 50 diesel-electrics arrived.

Bridging the distinction between its locomotives and adjacent carriage activities, Old Oak Common also cared for diesel multiple-units including the Metro-Cammell 'Blue Pullman' sets and the Gloucester RCW diesel parcels railcars Nos W55991/2.

So, what exactly was Old Oak Common's heyday? From the moment it opened, when the splendid De Glehn 'Compound' 4-4-2 No 102 *La France* was posed for photographs in 'the factory', it was the GWR's prestige depot and from then until the end of steam its importance was really unchallenged on the WR. But, with new purpose-built diesel depots at places such as Bristol Bath Road and Plymouth Laira, Old Oak Common was less in the limelight.

Even recently, in the fervour that surrounded the last months of the Class 50s, Old Oak very much played second fiddle to Laira.

To those of us who knew the Western Region around 1960 the period five years either side of that is fondly remembered. Old Oak then had a whole array of steam classes plus the latest diesels, including the glamorous 'Blue Pullmans' and the multi-coloured 'Westerns'. A day spent train-spotting a few miles west of Old Oak Common in 1962 would find a tremendous array of traffic. Most front-line expresses were in the hands of 'Warship' diesels of the D800 series, apart from the Worcester line trains which were the preserve of 'Castle' 4-6-0s. I remember that, when we first saw *Western Enterprise* in its desert sand livery, we thought it was still in undercoat!

Though Southall depot handled some of the freight workings, others involved locomotives working to or from Old Oak and these could produce 'Castles', 'Halls', 2-8-0s or the new BR Standard '9F' 2-10-0s. The 'Blue Pullmans' worked up to London in the morning and returned in the afternoon, in order to give business travellers a full day in London. Only the South Wales and Bristol workings passed south of Old Oak, and the Bristol route was sufficiently short that the unit could manage a mid-day return trip Paddington-Bristol-Paddington.

The steam/diesel period is also the period best covered by colour slide photography, and it was the publisher's request that this volume should be all colour.

I have divided the subject into three sections dealing with Old Oak Common depot, the three-mile stretch of main line between the depot and Paddington, and finally, the terminus itself. Though the bulk of the content is steam, there is an appropriate number of diesel views depicting much-loved classes. With the lifting of the ban on preserved diesels operating over BR it can only be a matter of time before a hydraulic is again heard screaming its way out of Paddington — indeed it may happen before these words appear in print. When it does, how fitting a tribute it would be to Old Oak Common, if the locomotive was 'Western' No D1015 *Western Champion*, the golden ochre example lovingly rebuilt and cared for by the staff of 81A.

Chris Leigh
Oundle,
Northants
1992

Acknowledgements

This book would not have been possible without the support of a number of photographers who were willing to loan their valuable and irreplaceable transparencies. More than half the content is the work of R. C. Riley and it is only fitting, therefore, that his name should appear with equal billing to mine. I merely made a selection (from more than 120 of Dick's transparencies as well as many others) and wrote the words. Thanks must also go to T. B. Owen who lent me all his Old Oak pictures, and to Mike Mensing, Peter Gray, Michael Farr, M. H. Yardley, D. G. Jones, Brian Roberts and Geoff Rixon for delving into their excellent collections on my behalf and to Richard Strange for proof and data checking.

Right:
'King' 4-6-0 No 6011 *King James I* stands outside Old Oak Common running shed, having been coaled and made ready to take a return special working, apparently in connection with the FA Cup Final, on 5 May 1956. The chalked inscription on the smokebox door 'Manchester 5, Birmingham Nil' was correct in sentiment if a trifle wide of the mark. Manchester City beat Birmingham 3-1 though one would have thought that the 'King', coming from the West Midlands, might have borne a more loyal inscription for one of its local teams! This locomotive carries the double chimney and improved draughting which had been the subject of much experimentation on the Western Region. *R. C. Riley*

Left:
Board meeting. The Great Western seldom used train headboards and only the unfortunate 'Cheltenham Flyer' was regularly adorned with a large board proclaiming it 'The World's Fastest Train'. It was BR which developed the publicity value of named train headboards from the early 1950s on the WR. The first boards were plain cast plates in BR standard shape with Gill Sans lettering. Those seen here are the much more elaborate versions produced by the WR when a little more regional autonomy was permitted from the mid-1950s. The 'Cathedrals Express' linked Paddington with Oxford, Worcester and Hereford, the 'Cheltenham Spa Express' served Gloucester and Cheltenham, and the 'Red Dragon', Swansea and Cardiff. The photograph was taken at Ranelagh Bridge on 12 March 1958. *R. C. Riley*

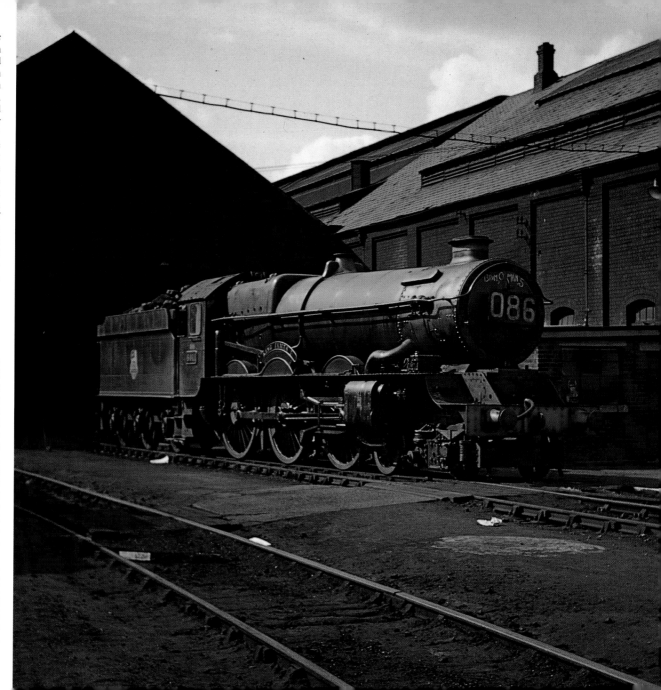

Above:
In contrast, Hawksworth 'County' 4-6-0 No 1015 *County of Gloucester* was not an Old Oak Common engine, and wears the 83D shed plate of Plymouth Laira. It is standing near the entrance to the depot from the main lines. The 'County' class were the Great Western's final 4-6-0 design and the only main line class designed by Hawksworth. A two-cylinder 'mixed traffic' type, they had initially worn the BR lined black livery. No 1000, the first of the class, was the subject of experiments with a distinctive design of double-chimney, but No 1015 carries the pattern eventually adopted for the class and looks handsome in the final style of BR lined green livery on 15 March 1959. *Bill Potter*

Above:
A bleak, chilly scene highlights the modern lines of the 'County' design as personified by No 1011 *County of Chester* at Old Oak Common on 2 February 1963 while allocated to Bristol St Philips Marsh. No 1011 was destined to be the last of its class, and though wearing final BR livery it was adorned with its number in Great Western style on the front buffer beam in its final weeks. In this condition the author was privileged to ride behind it between Wolverhampton Low Level and Shrewsbury on a Talyllyn RPS special in September 1964 just before the locomotive's withdrawal. *Geoff Rixon*

Above:
The prototype of the 330-strong 'Hall' class was No 4900 *Saint Martin*, rebuilt by Collett from 'Saint' No 2925 in 1924 and renumbered in 1928. Wearing the early BR mixed traffic lined black livery, it stands at Old Oak Common in September 1956. For part of its career it had been an 81A loco-motive and was allocated there at Nationalisation in 1948. In the background can be seen a visiting Stanier '8F' 2-8-0, and the depot's breakdown crane. *R. C. Riley*

Above:

Progressing down through the main line classes in evidence at 81A, we come to the Great Western's very trim mixed traffic type, the 'Grange' 4-6-0. The class is represented here by No 6842 *Nunhold Grange* of Bristol St Philips Marsh depot. Built at Swindon in 1937, this 'Grange' used wheels and motion from a withdrawn 'Mogul' and the tender from 'Saint' No 2908 *Lady of Quality*. Named after a private house near Warwick, the locomotive is in mint condition in this June 1957 view, as it had recently visited Swindon works for Heavy General overhaul, being released back to traffic on 21 May 1957. *R. C. Riley*

Above:
The 'Collett Goods' or '2251' class 0-6-0 was a type more generally associated with rural branch goods and cross-country lightweight passenger services. However, Old Oak Common did have one or two on its allocation from time to time, and others would occasionally arrive on local trip workings. By August 1959, when this view of No 2253 was taken, few had received the green livery which they later wore, and this one is in filthy black with the early lion-and-wheel emblem. No 2253 was new to traffic in March 1930 and was withdrawn from Worcester shed exactly 35 years later. *R. C. Riley*

Above:
Old Oak Common had its own substantial allocation of pannier tanks for a variety of local workings as well as the empty coaching stock turns between the carriage sidings and Paddington. No 9400 was the prototype of Hawksworth's heavy shunting design and was built at Swindon in 1947. It is seen here on shed standing alongside one of its predecessors, No 8773 of the Collett '57xx' class on October 25 1959. Both wear 81A shed codes. Despite being more modern than many of the pannier tanks which outlasted it, No 9400 was withdrawn two months later, in December 1959, to be preserved as part of the National Collection and is displayed in the Great Western Railway Museum at Swindon. *T. B. Owen*

Above:
A splendid portrait of an Old Oak Common pannier tank, '57xx' class 0-6-0PT No 9659, on 27 August 1961. These locomotives never wore BR green livery and this example portrays the final style of black livery and crest with painted cast iron numberplates and totally lacking in embellishments. By no means all GWR locomotives wore brass and copper decoration! No 9659 was built at Swindon in 1946. In the background is stark contrast in coal wagons, a new steel-bodied 16-ton mineral wagon alongside a much earlier wooden-bodied ex-private owner.
T. B. Owen

Above:
A type specifically associated with Old Oak Common was the 11 locomotives of the '97xx' class, Nos 9700-10, which were '57xx' 0-6-0PTs equipped with condensing apparatus. This reduced smoke and steam emissions by diverting the exhaust back through the water tank and was necessary for locomotives operating through tunnels to the GWR Smithfield goods depot. All these locomotives were allocated to Old Oak Common and No 9710 is particularly interesting in that it still sports the GWR roundel ('shirt button') livery on 15 March 1959.
Bill Potter

Above:
A livery contrast in this small class is represented by
No 9704 in BR livery with the small lion-and-wheel
emblem, five years earlier, in November 1954. On
the right is the cab and tender of No 4702, the only
one of the '47xx' 2-8-0s to receive the mixed traffic
lined black livery. *R. C. Riley*

Above:
Despite the Western Region's rush to apply elaborate green livery to every possible class in the late 1950s, before that there were few livery variations. One, apparently unjustified, example was the application of mixed traffic lined black livery to about half a dozen '57xx' 0-6-0PTs including No 8763, very much a goods and shunting engine, seen here at Old Oak in November 1954. The Old Oak '57xx' locomotives did, however, see use on ECS trains to and from Paddington, so perhaps this led to its 'mixed traffic' status. *R. C. Riley*

Above:
By August 1959 No 8763 had lost its lined black livery and is here seen heading a line-up of eight pannier tanks on the 'wrong' side of the coaling stage. The small bunkers of the tanks were not coaled from the overhead 'tubs' but from staithes or direct from wagons on one side of the coaling stage. However, on this occasion the coal had been delivered to the wrong side. Note the wooden-bodied wagons, including one still bearing a private owner name. In this view towards Paddington, the main line is beyond the coaches stabled on the right. *R. C. Riley*

Above:
Hawksworth's impressive short-wheelbase '15xx' class 0-6-0PTs were introduced in 1949 for heavy shunting and dockyard work. However, 81A had an allocation for empty stock working into Paddington, and this is the duty for which they are best remembered. No 1505, photographed on shed in May 1956, is unusual in having lined black livery (No 1503 also carried this livery). These locomotives proved extremely capable on the ECS workings, being well able to accelerate heavy trains, and occasionally to provide rear-end assistance to departing expresses. *R. C. Riley*

Above:
Moving inside Old Oak Common shed we find a group of four different tanks gathered around one of the four turntables. The foreground shows clearly how the turntable 'pit' area was completely covered. The four locomotives standing idle are '61xx' 2-6-2T No 6135, a type used on suburban passenger workings as well as ECS, condensing '97xx' 0-6-0PT No 9705, '15xx' 0-6-0PT No 1507 and '57xx' 0-6-0PT No 8757. *T. B. Owen*

Above:
A good angle on '97xx' 0-6-0PT No 9710 reposing inside the shed on 7 April 1963, with a couple of '28xx' 2-8-0s lurking in the shadows beyond. The pannier is parked, dead, over a pit and beneath one of the massive smoke chutes. The locomotive cabside carries the 'blue spot' and 'C' markings which were the GWR identifications for weight restriction and power classification respectively. A painted cast iron numberplate is carried, together with the later-pattern BR crest. *T. B. Owen*

Left:

Through skylights in the massive roof, shafts of light catch a Churchward 'Star' 4-6-0 No 4061 *Glastonbury Abbey* on 25 September 1955. The four-cylinder 'Stars' were G. J. Churchward's ultimate GWR passenger class and were built over a period from 1907 until 1923. No 4061 was new in May 1922 and was withdrawn in March 1957. Though it has the larger Collett tender, it is readily distinguished from its successors, the 'Castle' class, by the spartan Churchward cab with no side windows. *T. B. Owen*

Above right:

Moving from the shed itself, we find a number of locomotives under repair in 'the factory', Old Oak Common's repair shop, on 11 March 1962. At the extreme left, with red front numberplate, and wheels out, is Southall-based '63xx' 2-6-0 No 6385. 'Castle' No 7017 *G. J. Churchward* (81A) has had its bogie run out for attention and still carries 'The InterCity' headboard of its last Wolverhampton-Paddington working before admission to the shop. On the right is 'King' No 6023 *King Edward II*. This locomotive was consigned to Woodhams, Barry on withdrawal, rescued and stored at Bristol before going to the GWS at Didcot where restoration is taking place. *T. B. Owen*

Right:

Before the widespread arrival of diesel multiple-units around 1960, the Paddington-Reading suburban services were largely in the hands of the '61xx' 2-6-2Ts. These 'large Prairies' were a development of the '5101' class with 25psi extra boiler pressure to give them a little extra power for the intensive stop-start service. After dieselisation they survived on empty stock, parcels and local freight duties, and two of the class, Nos 6125 and 6163 are seen inside Old Oak Common shed on 8 March 1964.
Bill Potter

23

Above:

An interesting view inside Old Oak Common shed in September 1964 is dominated by modified 'Hall' 4-6-0 No 6974 *Bryngwyn Hall,* one of the '6959' class. The main modifications are evident in the plate framed bogie, mainframing visible above the front buffer beam, and the flat-sided 4,000-gallon tender. Behind the 'Hall' is Brush Type 4 diesel-electric No D1733, the locomotive which powered the 'XP64' train of prototype passenger stock and was the first to appear in the corporate 'rail blue' livery. For display purposes it carried double-arrow logos on red stickers on the cabsides, but these were removed immediately after its press launch.

R. C. Riley

Above:
The opposite extreme in diesel traction. Great Western AEC railcar No W31W peeps from the carriage shed at Old Oak Common and provides a good comparison between its carmine and cream livery, and the maroon carriage livery applied to the ex-GWR restaurant car alongside. The railcars worked suburban branches. including West Ealing-Greenford and West Drayton-Uxbridge/Staines West from the early 1950s when there were footplate crew shortages in the area, until the arrival of the new DMUs in 1958. This view dates from September 1958, shortly before the ex-GWR cars left the London area to see out their final months working from Worcester. *R. C. Riley*

Left:
Immaculate 'Grange' 4-6-0 No 6823 *Oakley Grange* spent much of March and April 1962 under Heavy General Overhaul at Swindon, returning to its home shed at Wolverhampton Oxley by 3 May 1962. Its appearance at Old Oak Common, recorded by the photographer as 'April' 1962, suggests that it had worked up from Swindon on a round-about journey home. It had cost just under £5,000 to build in January 1937, using wheels, motion and tender from a withdrawn 'mogul'. It seems incredible that this pristine locomotive saw only three more years' service, being withdrawn from Oxley in June 1965 and broken up at Birds, Swansea. *Geoff Rixon*

Right:
The Western Region had a number of the impressive Riddles 'WD' 2-8-0s on its books for heavy freight work. At Nationalisation, the regional total was no fewer than 89, of which eight were allocated to 81A. By 1 December 1956 the total was down to 47 on the Western Region. No 90355 was locally-based at Southall (81C) and is seen here at Old Oak Common in September 1956 having brought the locomotive coal train up from Rogerstone in South Wales. *R. C. Riley*

Above:
The mainstay of heavy freight power on the Western Region was the fleet of '28xx' 2-8-0s inherited from the GWR, a design which dated from 1903. No 2875 is typical of the original Churchward locomotives though it has the later curved framing. At Old Oak Common on 15 March 1959 it is sandwiched between a pair of the more modern BR Standard '9F' 2-10-0s introduced in 1954, the rear one being No 92241. *Bill Potter*

Above:
The pride of Old Oak's freight fleet was undoubtedly the small class of '47xx' 2-8-0s designed by Churchward for fast freight and introduced in 1919. Only one ever appeared in BR freight black livery, otherwise they were always afforded the full passenger lined green and even enjoyed a spell of use on passenger turns. No 4704 was the second to receive green livery and in October 1957 it had been specially cleaned for the photographer. It was photographed in the open and then moved to the carriage sidings, flanges protesting loudly on the curves, at the suggestion of its over-enthusiastic driver. It emerged from this siding much more gingerly than it went in! *R. C. Riley*

Above:

Four years later, No 4704 was in a much more scruffy state, standing over the ash pit on 27 August 1961. These 2-8-0s were a stretched version of the successful '43xx' mogul, having an extra set of 5ft 8in driving wheels and a much larger boiler. Over the years the Collett 4,000 gallon tenders were added and the straight back of the Churchward cab roof was extended to give the crew more protection. These very large locomotives had to have a modified design of chimney and safety valve bonnet to bring them within the loading gauge. It is a great pity that none survive in preservation. *T. B. Owen*

Above:
The final, largest and most modern freight design to be seen at Old Oak Common was the BR standard '9F' 2-10-0. Of this large class, a number were allocated to the Western Region for heavy freight work, particularly between South Wales and the Midlands and London. No 92247 had a short working life, having been new to traffic in December 1958 and withdrawn in October 1966. It is seen at Old Oak Common on 15 March 1959. *Bill Potter*

Left:
The last '9F' 2-10-0 to be built, though not the highest number, was No 92220 which, because it was also the last steam locomotive built for BR, received the name *Evening Star*. The locomotive was built at Swindon and the name was very much in the Swindon tradition, as was the decision to fit a coppercapped double-chimney. No 92220 was the only named member of its class and the only '9F' to carry full lined green passenger livery. It did perform a number of passenger duties during its allocation to the Western Region including passenger turns over the Somerset & Dorset line. It is seen here at Old Oak Common in April 1960 before taking out a Locomotive Club of Great Britain special train, its first duty in traffic apart from running-in turns. It was withdrawn after a working life of only five years but has since performed sterling work in preservation as part of the National Collection.
R. C. Riley

Right:
A worthy candidate for preservation was the last survivor of Churchward's celebrated 'Star' class 4-6-0s, No 4056 *Princess Margaret*. The locomotive is seen at Old Oak Common in September 1956 before taking out a Talyllyn Railway Preservation Society Special train from Paddington. A distinctive feature, clearly seen in this view is the 'elbow' steam pipe to the cylinder. Built with inside steam pipes, many 'Stars' later received the 'elbow' type before these were replaced by the more normal pattern similar to those on the 'Castle' 4-6-0s. When it came to preservation, No 4056 was passed over in favour of No 4003 *Lode Star* which was restored to more original condition and coupled to an earlier small tender for display at Swindon Railway Museum. In 1992 it was transferred to the NRM, York. *R. C. Riley*

Left:
Two celebrities stand at Old Oak Common in April 1960. Great Western 4-4-0 No 3440 *City of Truro* leads Caledonian Railway 4-2-2 No 123 following their display at Swindon during the naming of *Evening Star.* No 3440 was one of the double-framed 4-4-0s built during the William Dean/G. J. Churchward period at Swindon. On 9 May 1904, while heading an 'Ocean Mails' special between Plymouth and Bristol, *City of Truro* wrote its way into the history books with a very fast run down Wellington bank. A speed of 102mph was claimed - the first time 100mph had been achieved on rails. Ever since, devotees of other railway companies have endeavoured to prove that the claim was bogus, but their estimates still put the little 4-4-0 at so close to 'the ton' that it really makes no difference. Whatever the truth, it did ensure that this beautiful Victorian machine escaped destruction. *R. C. Riley*

Right:
This long straight shed at Old Oak Common was used to house and service the three eight-car diesel Pullman trains introduced in 1960. Built by Metro-Cammell, with a diesel-electric power car at either end, they bore similarities in concept to the present IC125 trains. The leading cab of one of the sets can be seen in this view inside what is still known as the 'Pullman shed'. Nowadays it serves as a paint shop and houses the breakdown train and other departmental equipment. On the right stands 'Castle' 4-6-0 No 4073 *Caerphilly Castle*, in this 2 June 1961 view. *R. C. Riley*

Above:

This view is a sequel to the previous one, for we can now see the reason for No 4073 being stabled under cover with the Pullman sets on 2 June 1961. The 'Castle' had been withdrawn from traffic and Swindon had restored it to original livery with a small tender for preservation. It is seen outside Paddington, being manoeuvred into position by a diesel shunter ready for the ceremony during which it was handed over to Sir David Follett, Director of the Science Museum. It remains to this day on static display in the museum in South Kensington. *R. C. Riley*

Above:

Out on the main line a 'Castle' is seen in full cry. No 5057 *Earl Waldegrave* is just minutes away from Old Oak Common as it passes Ealing Broadway with an express for Paddington in May 1961. Ealing Broadway is the first large station out of Paddington but is normally only a stop for local services. London Transport Central and District Line tube trains terminate there and the station, heavily rebuilt by the Great Western and BR over the years comes into its own if there is any need to terminate trains short of Paddington. No 5057 was one of the 'Castles' which received the 'Earl' nameplates transferred from the '90xx' 4-4-0s when the noble personages complained about their names being applied to small locomotives.

37

Above:
There was heavy traffic in empty coaching stock working between Paddington and the servicing and stabling sidings at Old Oak Common and in order to minimise disruption of the main line, a separate pair of carriage roads were provided which enabled stock to and from platforms on the 'departure' side to avoid crossing the main line on the level. These lines climbed away from the terminus and crossed a flyover to reach Old Oak Common. Large 'Prairie' 2-6-2T No 6124 is seen climbing from the depot towards the flyover on 19 October 1963. *T. B. Owen*

Above:
Moments later No 6124 can be seen approaching the flyover, with the main lines passing in the foreground. BR photographic permits allowed a degree of freedom which is no longer possible! The brown and cream livery carried by the leading corridor brake second (BSK) vehicle was applied in the mid-1950s to several rakes of BR Mk1 coaches for the Western Region's prestige named expresses. By this time, maroon was standard and the remaining brown and cream vehicles were scattered through a number of maroon sets. *T. B. Owen*

Left:
Empty stock workings were by no means always handled by the Old Oak tank engines. Main line locomotives frequently worked in and out of the terminus with empty coaches particularly when the stock was being removed from Paddington for stabling further down the line. Immaculate Worcester 'Castle' No 5037 *Monmouth Castle* does the job tender-first in October 1957, providing a splendid opportunity to catch the 1950s green livery and crest on film. Though built in 1935, the single-chimney engine has received one of the later Hawksworth welded 4,000 gallon tenders. *R. C. Riley*

Above:
Large 'Prairie' 2-6-2T No 6133 is seen approaching the flyover on 11 April 1964. *R. C. Riley*

Left:
An unusual view looking across the main lines towards the engine and carriage roads flyover. 'Castle' 4-6-0 No 7017 *G. J. Churchward* passes overhead as the passenger stock on the main line gives an interesting comparison of LMS Stanier (left) and GWR Collett (right) coaching stock. No 7017 was one of the postwar batch of 'Castles' completed in August 1948 and therefore coupled from the outset to a Hawksworth tender.
R. C. Riley

Right:
'King' 4-6-0 No 6025 *King Henry III* makes an imposing sight as it coasts gently along the up engine and carriage line between Old Oak Common and Paddington in August 1960. The unusual 'King' bogie is clearly seen. These bogies caused the entire class to be 'stopped' for a while during the 1950s after one suffered a failure which caused it to derail. 'Foreign' classes from other regions had to be drafted in to cope with the WR traffic during their absence.
R. C. Riley

Above:

On the final few miles into Paddington an up express passes the large goods depot at Westbourne Park, behind 'Western' Type 4 diesel-hydraulic No D1035 *Western Yeoman* in October 1963. The 'Western' was Swindon's final fling in designing a main line diesel-hydraulic locomotive for express passenger and freight use. The result was a classic locomotive which conformed to the profile of the Mk1 coaches and, eventually, wore matching maroon livery. However, to begin with there were experiments with 'Desert Sand', green and golden ochre colour schemes. The locomotive seen here is one of the batch built at Crewe, the first of which were turned out in unlined locomotive green. The goods depot has given way to the elevated 'Westway' road and a depot for buses! *R. C. Riley*

Above:
A marvellously evocative West London scene of the 1960s. Beyer-Peacock 'Hymek' Type 3 diesel-hydraulic No D7020 of Bristol Bath Road depot heads west from Paddington at Subway Junction near Westbourne Park, with a long parcels train. Note the early colour light signals on traditional GWR semaphore posts. The then-new apartment block in the background was demolished when the A40M 'Westway' road was constructed. The 'Hymek' was a diesel replacement for the 'Hall' 4-6-0 but was frequently pressed into front line pas- senger service on 'King' and 'Castle' duties to South Wales before the 'Westerns' arrived. 'Hymeks' were to be masters of Paddington-Oxford-Worcester-Hereford passenger services during much of the mid-1960s and Old Oak had its own alloca- tion from the 101-strong class. *R. C. Riley*

Above:
The magnificent Churchward '47xx' 2-8-0s were built for fast freight work, but when pressed into passenger service they were stalwart performers. During the summer holiday period the Western Region carried heavy traffic to and from South West England and motive power staff were hard-pressed to supply the necessary locomotives. For one summer, during 1958, Old Oak '47xxs' had a regular Saturday passenger diagram which included the down 'Royal Duchy' express. The impeccable turn-out of No 4708 and its all brown and cream Mk1 stock on 30 August 1958 amply demonstrates that even at this time BR could present a train at least as good-looking as any pre-1948 company. *R. C. Riley*

Above:
Paddington approaches are spanned by five road bridges, at least three with curved girder spans, Ranelagh Bridge, Westbourne Bridge and Bishops Bridge Road, the last named being close to the platform ends. Setting out for the west, 'Hall' 4-6-0 No 4962 *Ragley Hall* passes under Ranelagh Bridge while marshalling a parcels train. The leading vehicle is a Great Western 'Siphon H' van originally built for milk churn and parcels traffic. This is a fairly early outside-framed version of the design, the 'H' having a higher roof profile than the better-known 'Siphon G' design. *R. C. Riley*

49

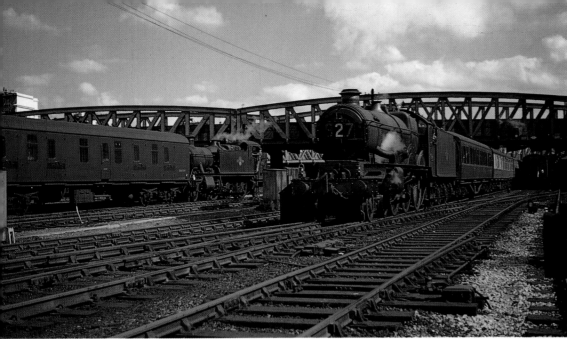

Above:

Despite nationalisation in 1948 Swindon continued to build locomotives to traditional GWR style, complete with number-plates on the cab-side, though the painted figures on the bufferbeam were replaced by the cast version on the smokebox in the Midland and LMS style. The first 'Castle' to be withdrawn was No 100A1 *Lloyds* (from 81A in March 1950), whilst in August the last of the long line of 'Castle' class 4-6-0 locomotives was produced; appropriately named *Swindon*, the locomotive is seen here. No 7037 *Swindon* was withdrawn in March 1963 having completed just over half a million miles in service. *R. C. Riley*

Above:
Southall '14xx' 0-4-2T No 1420 stands in for a failed diesel-mechanical parcels railcar in June 1959. It is seen pulling away from Paddington's parcels depot alongside platform 1 (more recently used as a passenger platform, No 1A). The '14xx' tanks allocated to Southall worked the West Ealing-Greenford, and West Drayton-Uxbridge Vine Street/Staines West branch push-pull services together with the larger '54xx' 0-6-0PTs and diesel railcars. *R. C. Riley*

Owing to the distance between Paddington and Old Oak Common, a separate servicing depot was provided at Ranelagh Road, close to the terminus, to enable a much more rapid turn-round of main line locomotives. It was provided with routine servicing, coaling, watering and turning facilities and remained in use until the early 1980s as a diesel servicing point. Double-chimney 'King' 4-6-0 No 6006 *King George I* is being turned in the tightly confined little depot during March 1957.
R. C. Riley

Right:
In August 1960 the turntable at a packed Ranelagh Road servicing depot is being aligned ready to release a 'King' 4-6-0 from the sidings. Alongside it are 'Castles' and 'Kings', and in the background, a BR Standard 'Britannia' 4-6-2. The latter were mainly used on South Wales services.
R. C. Riley

Above:
Paddington, in steam days, was a dark, dirty place and seemed set in a pit surrounded by black buildings. The station throat opened into daylight with the black corrugated Paddington Goods station to the north and these grim black structures to south, above the Departures Signalbox and the parcels depot seen here. Hawksworth '15xx' 0-6-0PT No 1504 was on empty stock duties in 1962.
Geoff Rixon

Above:
Sporting full Swindon green livery, copper and brass fittings, a '61xx' 2-6-2T makes a lively start away from the terminus with empty stock. Built for local passenger services from Paddington, the locomotive has been displaced from these duties by the Pressed Steel three-car diesel units, one of which is passing in the background. Designed for a service life of 15 years or so, from 1960, these units (as Class 117) still work the Paddington-Reading locals in 1992.
T. B. Owen

Left:
Against the backdrop of Paddington Goods Depot, Hawksworth '15xx' 0-6-0PT No 1503 brings the empty stock for a Worcester express into the terminus on 17 August 1963. An example of the GWR colour light signalling can be seen on the left and beyond the train is one of the company's standard conical water tanks. *T. B. Owen*

Right:
One of Old Oak Common's other Hawksworth panniers, '84xx' 0-6-0PT No 9420 stands at the platform end having followed a departing express down the platform. It will then wait for the road back to the Old Oak carriage sidings unless required to remove stock from an adjacent platform. There was always a healthy number of 'spotters' here at the end of Platform 9. *Geoff Rixon*

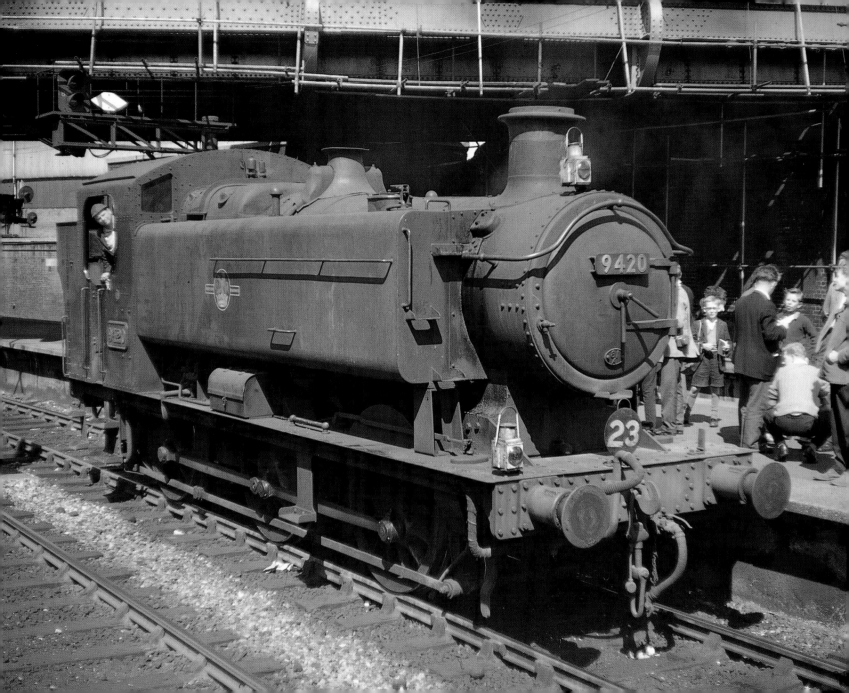

Left:
Old Oak 'Castle' No 4082 *Windsor Castle* drifts into Paddington with an up express in July 1962. Despite its 'early' number this locomotive dates from July 1948, when it was completed as No 7013 *Bristol Castle* in experimental apple green livery. When King George VI died in 1952 No 4082 was required for the funeral train, as it had performed the same duty for the previous King. However, it was not considered to be in good enough condition at the time, so its name and numberplates were transferred to No 7013. It never reverted to its correct identity.
Geoff Rixon

Right:
The Paddington of fond memory for enthusiasts of my generation! Even the Morris Royal Mail van standing on the cab road is absolutely typical of the period. 'Warship' B-B diesel-hydraulic No D843 *Sharpshooter* stands alongside Old Oak 'Castle' No 5070 *Sir Daniel Gooch* under Brunel's splendid roof. Both have arrived on up expresses and the 'Warship' already wears a tail lamp, ready to follow its empty stock out of the terminus.
T. B. Owen

Above:

The detail of Matthew Digby-Wyatt's ironwork frames 'Castle' 4-6-0 No 7000 *Viscount Portal*, named after the last Chairman of the Great Western Railway. No 7000 was built in 1946 and was allocated to Newton Abbot until transferred to Gloucester in 1959 and Worcester in 1963, from where it was withdrawn in December that year. At the time of this view on 16 November 1963 it was just weeks from withdrawal, and had brought in an express from Worcester. *T. B. Owen*

Above:
A delightful 'stop-blocks' scene at Paddington on 19 October 1963, '84xx' 0-6-0PTs Nos 8481 and 9435 having brought in empty stock. In the background, one of the suburban Pressed Steel three-car diesel units wears the original unlined dark green livery. Standing on platform five are two of the portable safes used for transporting official documents between Paddington 'head office' and outlying stations in the London area. *T. B. Owen*

Above:
One of my favourite views in this volume is this shot of the Western Region's Blue Pullman trains on their inaugural day, 12 September 1960. Three eight-car units were supplied to the WR by Metro-Cammell, one each for the new 'Bristol Pullman' and 'Birmingham Pullman' services and another to replace locomotive-haulage on the existing 'South Wales Pullman'. Their distinctive Nanking blue and white livery and the 90mph top speed of the twin power cars made them a major attraction during the early 1960s. Application of yellow ends, then later the awful grey livery took them into decline and when HSTs came along they were swiftly consigned for scrap lest they should cause confusion. The white-coated drivers (seen here) earned the uncomplimentary nick-name 'Ice cream men'.
Michael Farr

Above:
Two sailors consult their map as 'King' 4-6-0 No 6009 *King Charles II* stands with the up 'Cambrian Coast Express' on 6 July 1962. This express from Aberystwyth and Pwllheli was worked from Wolverhampton by 'Kings' until dieselisation from the end of the 1962 summer timetable. At that time only Nos 6000/5/11/18/25/28 were left in traffic and from 10 September 1962 most Paddington-Wolverhampton services were diesel-hauled. *Geoff Rixon*

Above:
A locomotiveman smiles for the camera as he poses with 'King' No 6016 *King Edward V* at Paddington. The Old Oak 'King' was about to depart with the 6.08pm to Wrexham (extended from Wolverhampton) on Friday, 8 June 1962. *Michael Mensing*

Right:
Parting shot — or so it looks. In fact 'King' 4-6-0 No 6007 *King William III* is negotiating the crossovers as it reverses into Paddington to pick up a down express on 18 August 1962. *Geoff Rixon*

Left:
After the Old Oak shed buildings had gone, the remaining turntable retained its wooden flooring, as seen here on 3 June 1967. Standing round the turntable is an array of diesel traction, surprisingly lacking a 'Western' or 'Warship'. 'Hymeks' Nos D7058 and D7056 sport original green and early blue liveries, respectively. Two of the NBL Type 2s used on ECS and local freight work, separate the 'Hymeks', while on the right are a pair of Brush Type 4s, Nos D1612 and D1721. As Class 47 the latter were to become the mainstay of WR locomotive power after the diesel-hydraulics had gone. *Bill Potter*

Above:
A little later, in August 1967, and the Brush Type 4s dominate the turntable group, together with another 'Hymek' No D7052 wearing the early blue livery with small yellow warning panel. Two of the green 'Brushes' have received full yellow ends. *D. G. Jones*

Above:
The 'Factory' at Old Oak Common, now converted for diesel traction and seen in August 1967 with 'Western', Brush '4', NBL Type 2, 'Hymek' and 'Warship' main line types, plus a 350hp diesel shunter in view. *D. G. Jones*

Right:
The NBL Type 2 diesel-hydraulics were generally not well thought of, but I always had a soft spot for them. They were associated with local traffic and china clay workings over the best of the Cornish branch lines, before several were transferred to Old Oak Common for empty stock working into Paddington. At Acton Yard they would take over the through Ripple Lane-Staines West oil tanks, from ER motive power. No D6327 reposes in the sun outside the 'Factory' wearing the early blue livery with small yellow warning panels. *D. G. Jones*

Left:
'Hymek' No D7045 shows its handsome design to
advantage in the early 'monastral' blue livery with
small yellow panel and off-white windscreen pillars
at Old Oak Common in August 1967. *D. G. Jones*

Right:
One of the last pre-Nationalisation items at Old Oak
Common must surely have been the breakdown
crane, Ransomes and Rapier No E8138 of 1939,
which was still operational at 81A in April 1983.
Though the current crane is a new 75ton diesel type,
the depot still stables a much earlier diesel perma-
nent way crane, the jib runner for which is a 1928-
built GWR vehicle! *Brian Roberts*

Above:
Old Oak traction as fondly remembered by the author — and all hydraulic. Two 'Hymek' type 3s stand outside the 'factory' with 'Westerns' Nos D1023 *Western Fusilier* (now preserved at the National Railway Museum, York) and D1000 *Western Enterprise,* the prototype of the class. No D1000 wears its original 'desert sand' livery but with the addition of yellow warning panels in this 11 April 1964 view. It always seemed to look more scruffy than the richer-coloured golden ochre of No D1015 *Western Champion.* On the right stands one of the diesel fuel tanks. The author was permitted to ascend the steps when visiting the depot in recent years to take photographs for an open day preview. Though quite small, it provides a commanding view of the whole depot, though largely against the sun at around mid-day. *R. C. Riley*

Above:
Old Oak Common depot buildings under demolition
in 1963. Earlier views in this volume show locomotives posed in this area. *R. C. Riley*

Above:
With diesel locomotives standing inside, part of Old Oak Common is demolished on 27 June 1965. The turntable has been cut up. What price the 'Iron Mink' van body in the foreground if it had survived?
T. B. Owen

Right:
Happier days recalled at Old Oak Common, with '47xx' No 4700 heading light engine to Paddington past the Old Oak Common Engine Shed box on 10 August 1957. *R. C. Riley*

Allocation at 21 March 1959

Class 15xx 0-6-0PT
1500   1503   1504   1505

Class 2251 0-6-0
2222   2276   2282

Class 57xx 0-6-0PT

3648	3688	3754	4615	4644	5717	5764
7722	7734	7791	8751	8753	8754	8756
8757	8759	8760	8761	8762	8763	8764
8765	8767	8768	8769	8770	8771	8772
8773	9658	9659	9661	9700	9701	9702
9703	9704	9705	9706	9707	9709	9710
9725	9751	9754	9758	9784		

'Castle' 4-6-0

4082 *Windsor Castle*	4090 *Dorchester Castle*
4096 *Highclere Castle*	5008 *Raglan Castle*
5014 *Goodrich Castle*	5027 *Farleigh Castle*
5034 *Corfe Castle*	5035 *Coity Castle*
5040 *Stokesay Castle*	5043 *Earl of Mount Edgcumbe*
5044 *Earl of Dunraven*	5052 *Earl of Radnor*
5056 *Earl of Powis*	5060 *Earl of Berkeley*
5065 *Newport Castle*	5066 *Sir Felix Pole*
5074 *Hampden*	5082 *Swordfish*
5084 *Reading Abbey*	5087 *Tintern Abbey*
5093 *Upton Castle*	7001 *Sir James Milne*
7004 *Eastnor Castle*	7008 *Avondale Castle*
7013 *Bristol Castle*	7017 *G. J. Churchward*
7024 *Powis Castle*	7025 *Sudeley Castle*
7027 *Thornbury Castle*	7030 *Cranbrook Castle*
7032 *Denbigh Castle*	7033 *Hartlebury Castle*
7036 *Taunton Castle*	

Class 47xx 2-8-0
4700   4701   4702   4704   4708

'Hall' 4-6-0

4900 *Saint Martin*	4919 *Donnington Hall*
5923 *Colston Hall*	5929 *Hanham Hall*
5931 *Hatherley Hall*	5932 *Haydon Hall*
5936 *Oakley Hall*	5939 *Tangley Hall*
5940 *Whitbourne Hall*	5941 *Campion Hall*
5954 *Faendre Hall*	5958 *Knolton Hall*
5976 *Ashwicke Hall*	5987 *Brocket Hall*
6920 *Barningham Hall*	6942 *Eshton Hall*
6959 *Peatling Hall*	6961 *Stedham Hall*
6962 *Soughton Hall*	6966 *Witchingham Hall*
6973 *Bricklehampton Hall*	6974 *Bryngwyn Hall*
6978 *Haroldstone Hall*	6990 *Witherslack Hall*
7902 *Eaton Mascot Hall*	7903 *Foremarke Hall*
7904 *Fountains Hall*	7927 *Willington Hall*

'King' 4-6-0

6000 *King George V*	6002 *King William IV*
6003 *King George IV*	6009 *King Charles II*
6012 *King Edward VI*	6013 *King Henry VIII*
6015 *King Richard III*	6018 *King Henry VI*
6019 *King Henry V*	6022 *King Edward III*
6023 *King Edward II*	6024 *King Edward I*
6028 *King George VI*	

Class 61xx 2-6-2T

6110	6111	6113	6120	6121	6132	6135
6141	6142	6144	6145	6149	6158	6159
6168						

Class 94xx 0-6-0PT

8434	8459	9400	9410	9411	9412	9414
9416	9418	9419	9420	9423	9479	

Class 9F 2-10-0

92229	92230	92238	92239	92240	92241
92244	92245	92246	92247		